E·Z Bock's Best

Volume V

CONTENTS

Almost every keyboard publication arranged by Fred Bock contains a foreword, which, due to their creative and humorous content, have become classics. The foreword below was written by Fred's long-time friend, Carl Farrer, and appeared in Bock's Best Volume II (BG0572) in 1982.

A LITTLE ABOUT BOCK[1], FRED[2]

1. Family name
2. First name, a diminutive of Alfred, which, according to the 2,094-page (plus xviii pages) *The Reader's Digest Great Encyclopedia Dictionary*, © 1966, means "Elf Counselor."

A brief aside to extrapolate little-known facts concerning elves: Elf is a contraction used by intimates of the legendary herbist, "Elfis of Parsely," who immortalized the little people in his biography, "Know Thy Elf." Lasting fame came, however, as he laid the herb aside to become a pianist and composer in the Franz Liszt tradition, arranging for the piano by ear. Some say that strains of his greatest hit, "What's It All About, Elfie," may still be heard if one walks through Irish woods when the mist is rising and the moon is full. In a pique of inspiration Elfis locked himself in his room only to emerge two days later with a Christmas oratorio masterpiece. Requesting permission to dedicate this new work to his close friend and mentor, King Elfred the Great, King Elfred counseled him, "Don't" - earning him the title Mighty Counselor.

Suffice to say that our own Fred Bock carries on in the same great tradition. I, myself, have heard him personally say to his office secretary in response to daily mail from those offering to send new compositions and arrangements, "Write all these people and make it Crystal-clear and tell them, 'Don't!'."

Unfortunately, space does not permit an exhausted listing of Fred's by-now well-known accomplishments, including conducting stints at Bel Air and Hollywood Presbyterian Churches, his fame as organist, pianist, composer, arranger, studio musician, former pianistic darling of Youth For Christ, workshop leader, auto-suggestor, and sense-of-humor person, nationally known as the Wit of Worship. Indulgence is asked (*Wittenburg Door* save your centerfold) for such a concise listing. This lack of space is truly bio-degradable. Purists and fans may obtain detailed information by purchasing any and all of the best-selling piano arrangement volumes by Fred Bock currently available in music stores across the nation.

For myself, thanks, Fred, for this chance to express my admiration and lauds. You're one of the fondest things I am of.

Carl Farrer

CARL FARRER

BE THOU MY VISION

Irish Folk Melody
Arranged by FRED BOCK
Adapted by LLOYD LARSON

17
21
a little brighter
mf
25
30
35

39
43
47
52
56
ten.
ten.

O GOD, OUR HELP IN AGES PAST

WILLIAM CROFT
Arranged by FRED BOCK
Adapted by LLOYD LARSON

21
ten.
ten.
25
rit.
Majestically
(bring out mel.)
f
29
32
35
f
ff
36
f
mf

MY FAITH LOOKS UP TO THEE

LOWELL MASON
Arranged by FRED BOCK
Adapted by LLOYD LARSON

17
mp
22
26
30
ten.
ten.
34
r.h.
l.h.

BLESSED ASSURANCE

PHOEBE P. KNAPP
Arranged by FRED BOCK
Adapted by LLOYD LARSON

13
f
16
19
mf
22
25
rit.
ten.
ten.
a tempo

28
30
32
34
rit.

WHILE SHEPHERDS WATCHED THEIR FLOCKS

GEORGE FRIDERIC HANDEL
Arranged by FRED BOCK
Adapted by LLOYD LARSON

12
15
18
21
f
24

27
f
30
33
36
39
rit.
ff

JESUS, THE VERY THOUGHT OF THEE

JOHN B. DYKES
Arranged by FRED BOCK
Adapted by LLOYD LARSON

25
ten.
ten.
pp
30
mp
35
40
45
rit.
mp

GOD SO LOVED THE WORLD

JOHN STAINER
Arranged by FRED BOCK
Adapted by LLOYD LARSON

17
21
26
dim.
mp
31
36
mp

41
rit.
a tempo
45
f
49
54
59

64
69
p
74
79
ten.
ten.
84
pp

TO GOD BE THE GLORY

WILLIAM H. DOANE
Arranged by FRED BOCK
Adapted by LLOYD LARSON

Brightly, but majestically

20
24
mf
28
p
32
f
ten.
ten.
ten.
ten.
ten.
ten.
36
rit. poco a poco
dim. poco a poco

JUST AS I AM

WILLIAM B. BRADBURY
Arranged by FRED BOCK
Adapted by LLOYD LARSON

Prayerfully and tenderly

25
30
35
ten.
ten.
39
44
mp
p
r.h.

FAIREST LORD JESUS

Silesian Folk Melody
Arranged by FRED BOCK
Adapted by LLOYD LARSON

16
a little stronger
mf
20
24
mf
mp
mf
28
mp
32
Flowing
mf

bring out melody
mf
p